A. P. [from old catalog] Potts

The Needle Workers' Guide without a Teacher

A. P. [from old catalog] Potts

The Needle Workers' Guide without a Teacher

ISBN/EAN: 9783744739207

Printed in Europe, USA, Canada, Australia, Japan

Cover: Foto ©Andreas Hilbeck / pixelio.de

More available books at **www.hansebooks.com**

THE
NEEDLE
WORKERS'

GUIDE

Without a Teacher.

An Entirely New Method of
Self-Instructions on

"ART NEEDLE=WORK,"

In which all the different stitches used in making
are thoroughly taught and explained by

DIAGRAMS, LETTERS & NUMBERS.
—INCLUDING ALSO—

A GUIDE TO KENSINGTON PAINTING

— BY —

A. P. POTTS,

Author of "The Needle-Worker's Lesson Sheet."

**REVISED
EDITION.**

W. T. LANGTON, PRINTER,
7104 South Chicago Avenue.
CHICAGO, ILL.

PREFACE.

The reason for the appearance of this book, "The Needle-Worker's Guide," may be said to be four fold. First—The absence of any such work that embraces within its scope in a plain methodical manner, the progressive stages of Art Needle-work, instructions commencing at the first principles, and carrying the learner forward, step by step, to a degree of perfection. Second—One of the most noticeable and interesting features of our times is the increasing tendency of the people toward the study and practice of the artistic, and the ardent desire expressed by many for a reasonable system of self-instructions. Third—To still further stimulate and encourage that tendency among the people, the fostering of which must have a decided, refining effect. Fourth—For a book (together with the Needle-Worker's Lesson Sheet accompanying it,) which would comprise and teach by the aid of diagrams, letters and figures, all the principal stitches used in Art Needle-Work. This plan possesses every advantage and is equal to personal instructions. These reasons, together with the numerous encouragements the author has received from a former publication, has induced him to undertake the task of a second publication.

The author claims for this book that by the plain and easy manner of teaching the learner how each separate stitch is made by lines, dots, letters and figures which is an entirely new method of teaching Art Needle-Work. The plain and simple manner in which the instructions are given for making decorative articles by this new method from the numerous full-size working patterns herein contained, will render the task of the learner both easy and simple.

The work has been explicitly written and carefully executed, and every possible means of descriptive and illustrative power utilized in order to make the work truly what the title page indicates, "The Needle-Worker's Guide."

The author claims for it, special usefulness, and hopes that it will be highly appreciated and trusts it will meet and deserve a wide acceptation at the hands of the innumerable ladies for whom it is intended, while it escapes what it does not court the hypercriticism of the pedant.

A. P. Potts.

Chicago, Ill., January, 1895.

LIST OF DIAGRAMS AND PATTERNS.

...TABLE OF CONTENTS...

...TABLE OF CONTENTS...

CONTINUED.

BORDER STITCH DIAGRAM AND PATTERN.

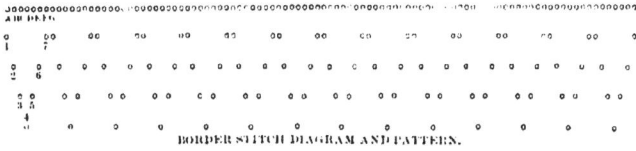

INSTRUCTIONS FOR MAKING BORDER STITCH.

Make a pattern from the engraving and stamp the design upon the material.

Hold the material so as to work from you. Bring the needle up from underneath through dot 1, (see above diagram,) insert it in dot A, bring it out in dot B, insert it in dot 2, bring it out in dot 3, insert it in dot C, bring it out in dot D, insert it in dot 4, bring it out in dot 5, insert it in dot E, bring it out in dot F, insert it in dot 6, bring it out in dot 7 and insert it in dot G. You have now finished one block. Continue the operation in the same manner until your work is completed.

The stem stitch is used for finishing the upper edge of the border. By using different shades of silk thread for each alternate block, a very beautiful effect can be produced.

A B C D E F G H K

BASKET STITCH DIAGRAM AND PATTERN.

INSTRUCTIONS FOR MAKING BASKET STITCH.

Make a pattern from the engraving and stamp the design upon the material.

Hold the material so that the needle will point to your left in working and bring the needle up from underneath through dot 1, (see above diagram,) insert it in dot C, bring it out in dot A, pulling the thread all the way through, insert it in dot 1, bring it out in dot 2, insert it in dot D, bring it out in dot B, insert it in dot 5, bring it out in dot 3, insert it in dot E, bring it out in dot C, insert it in dot 6, bring it out in dot 4, insert it in dot F, bring it out in dot D, insert it in dot 7, bring it out in dot 5, insert it in dot G, bring it out in dot E, insert it in dot 8, bring it out in dot 6, insert it in dot H, bring it out in dot F, insert it in dot 9, bring it out in dot 7, insert it in dot K, bring it out in dot G, and continue the operation in like manner by always inserting the needle one dot to the right of the last stitch and bringing the point out one dot to the left of the last stitch until your work is completed. This stitch is commonly used for borders and for work on thin and transparent materials.

Note. In transfering patterns from the above and foregoing designs herein contained, it is not necessary to copy the letters and figures, simply the dots and outlines.

BRICK STITCH DIAGRAM AND PATTERN.

INSTRUCTIONS FOR MAKING BRICK STITCH.

Make a pattern from the engraving and stamp the design upon the material.

To make the horizontal stitches representing the edge of the brick, bring the needle up from underneath through dot 1, (see above diagram,) thrust it down through dot 2, bring it up through dot 3, thrust it down through dot 4, bring it up through dot 5, thrust it down through dot 6, and continue in like manner until you have finished the horizontal stitches.

To make the vertical stitches representing the ends of the brick, bring the needle up underneath, through dot 1, thrust it down through dot 2, bring it up through dot 3, thrust it down through dot 4, bring it up through dot 5, thrust it down through dot 6, and continue in like manner until you have finished the vertical stitches.

To make the horizontal stitches, representing the seams between the brick, bring the needle up from underneath through dot A, thrust it down through dot B, bring it up through dot C, thrust it down through dot D, bring it up through dot E, thrust it down through dot D, bring it up through dot C, thrust it down through dot B, and continue in like manner until you have finished the horizontal stitches.

To make the vertical stitches representing the seams between the ends of the brick, bring the needle up from underneath through dot F, thrust it down through dot G, bring it up through dot H, thrust it down through dot B, bring it up through dot C, thrust it down through dot K and continue in like manner until your work is finished.

In making the horizontal and vertical stitches representing the seams between the brick, you should use a different colored silk thread from that used in making the stitches representing the brick in order to give the work the desired effect.

DIAMOND STITCH DIAGRAM AND PATTERN.

INSTRUCTIONS FOR MAKING DIAMOND STITCH.

Make a pattern from the engraving and stamp the design upon the material.

Bring the needle up from underneath through dot 1, (see above diagram,) thrust it down through dot 2, bring it up through dot 3, thrust it down through dot 4, bring it up through dot 5, thrust it down through dot 6, bring it up through dot 7, thrust it down through dot 8, bring it up through dot 9, thrust it down through dot 10, bring it up through dot 8, thrust it down through dot 10, bring it up through dot 9, thrust it down through dot 6, bring it up through dot 7, thrust it down through dot 4, bring it up through dot 5, thrust it down through dot 2, bring it up through dot 3, thrust it down through dot 1.

Continue the operation in like manner until your work is completed.

HERRING BONE STITCH DIAGRAM AND PATTERN.

INSTRUCTIONS FOR MAKING HERRING BONE STITCH.

Make a pattern from the engraving and stamp the design upon the material.

Bring the needle up from underneath through dot 1, (see above diagram,) thrust it down through dot 2, bring it up through dot 3, thrust it down through dot 4, bring it up through dot 5, thrust it down through dot 6, bring it up through dot 7, thrust it down through dot 8, bring it up through dot 9, thrust it down through dot 8, bring it up through dot 9, thrust it down through 10, bring it up through dot 11, thrust it down through dot 12, bring it up through dot 13, thrust it down through dot 14, bring it up through dot 15, thrust it down through dot 16, bring it up through dot 17, thrust it down through dot 16, bring it up through dot 17, thrust it down through dot 18, bring it up through dot 19, thrust it down through dot 20, bring it up through dot 21, thrust it down through dot 22, bring it up through dot 23, thrust it down through dot 24, and continue the operation in like manner until your work is finished.

This is a very popular stitch, making a good appearance and for this reason is adapted to a wide range of work. It is especially useful in taking the place of the unsightly ridge made by a fell and for joining seams, and it should be made with a very coarse silk thread.

For-get-me-not Petal Stitch Diagram and For-get-me-not Rose Pattern

INSTRUCTIONS FOR MAKING FORGET-ME-NOT PETAL STITCH.

To make this stitch and also the Forget-me-not Rose, thread a needle with two strands of silk and bring it up from underneath through dot 1, (see above diagram,) coil the thread around so as to cover the stamped outline of the petal as shown in the engraving, place the thumb of the left hand over the coil so as to hold it firmly in place while you thrust the needle down through the material where it was brought up and there fasten the thread.

For the purpose of fastening the petal upon the material, thread a needle with a single strand of silk and bring it up from underneath through dot 2 inside of the coil and thrust it down on the outside near where it was brought up and there fasten the thread. Proceed in like manner until all the petals are finished.

This stitch is used for the purpose of making the petals of other small flowers as well as those of the forget-me-not.

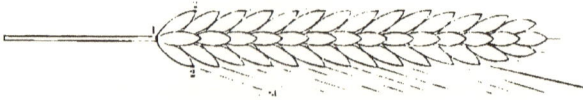

Wheat Grain Stitch Diagram and Wheat Head Pattern

INSTRUCTIONS FOR MAKING WHEAT GRAIN STITCH.

Make a pattern from the engraving and stamp the design upon the material.

Bring the needle up from underneath through dot 1, (see above diagram,) insert it in dot 2, and bring the point out in dot 1, allowing the needle to protrude about two-thirds of its length and with the right hand wind the thread around the point of the needle a sufficient number of times to cover the length of the grain indicated in the engraving, place the thumb of the left hand over the wound part and there hold it firmly until the needle and thread is drawn all the way through the coil, then thrust the needle down through dot 2, bring it up again through dot 1, insert it in dot 2, bring the point out in dot 1, allowing it to protrude about two-thirds of its length; wind the thread around the point of the needle as before and place the thumb over the wound part, draw the needle and thread all the way through the coil and thrust it down through dot 2 as before; this operation makes one grain.

To make the barbs, (those small delicate thread-like fibers that project from the point of the grains indicated by the engraving and which should be made with a much finer silk thread than that used for making the grains,) bring the needle up from underneath through dot 3, thrust it down between the coils through dot 2. You then have a grain of wheat completed in all parts. Proceed in like manner with the others until your work is finished. This stitch is also used for embroidering flowers having small petals and for small leaves.

INSTRUCTIONS FOR MAKING WHEAT HEAD.

Make a pattern from the engraving and stamp the design upon the material.

Commence at the bottom of the head and work alternately on either side to the top or point. To make the centre grains, which are made without barbs except the centre grain at the extreme point of the head, indicated by the engraving, commence at the top or point of the head and work to the bottom. Lastly make the barbs.

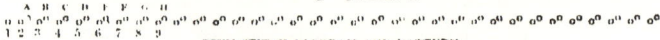

STEM STITCH DIAGRAM AND PATTERN.

INSTRUCTIONS FOR MAKING STEM STITCH.

Make a pattern from the engraving and stamp the design upon the material.

Hold the material so that figure one of the diagram will be to your left and bring the needle up from underneath through dot 1, (see above diagram,) insert it in dot A, (allowing the thread to drop toward you before inserting the needle,) bring it out in dot 2, insert it in dot B, bring it out in dot 3, insert it in dot C, bring it out in dot 4, insert it in dot D, bring it out in dot 5, insert it in dot E, bring it out in dot 6, insert it in dot F, bring it out in dot 7, insert it in dot G, bring it out in dot 8, insert it in dot H, bring it out in dot 9, and continue the operation in like manner by inserting the needle in the second dot next the last stitch and bringing it out in the first dot next the last stitch until your work is finished.

This stitch is used for making the stems of leaves, stems of wheat, golden rod sumach, forget-me-not and is also used for finishing the centre of the feather stitch and the upper edge of the border stitch.

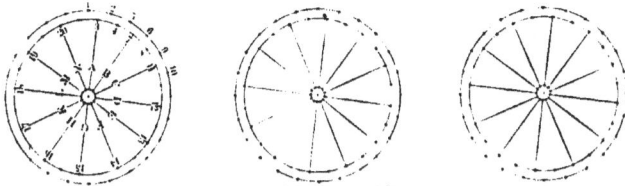

Wheel Stitch Diagram and Pattern

INSTRUCTIONS FOR MAKING WHEEL STITCH.

Make a pattern from the engraving and stamp the design upon the material. (In making the pattern it is not necessary to stamp the circle lines seen in the engraving simply the dots.) Bring the needle up from underneath through dot 1, (see above diagram,) thrust it down through dot 2, bring it up through dot 3, thrust it down through dot 4, bring it up through dot 2, thrust it down through dot 5, bring it up through dot 4, thrust it down through dot 7, bring it up through dot 5, thrust it down through dot 6, bring it up through dot 7, thrust it down through dot 8, bring it up through dot 6, thrust it down through dot 9, bring it up through dot 8, thrust it down through dot 11, bring it up through dot 9, thrust it down through dot 10, and continue to take the stitches in like manner until the rim is finished.

To make the spokes, use a different shade of silk thread from that used in making the rim in order to give the work a more beautiful effect, bring the needle up from underneath through dot 3, thrust it down through dot A, bring it up through dot B, thrust it down through dot 7, bring it up through dot 11, thrust it down through dot C, bring it up through dot D, thrust it down through dot 12, bring it up through dot 13, thrust it down through dot E, bring it up through dot F, thrust it down through dot 14, bring it up through dot 15, thrust it down through dot G, bring it up through dot H, thrust it down through dot 16, bring it up through dot 17, thrust it down through dot K, bring it up through dot L, thrust it down through dot 18, bring it up through dot 19, thrust it down through dot M, bring it up through dot N, and thrust it down through dot 20. You have now completed one wheel. Continue with the others in like manner until your work is finished.

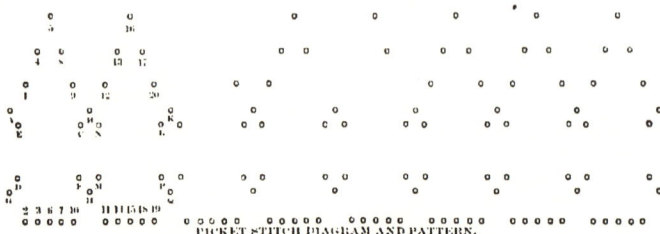

PICKET STITCH DIAGRAM AND PATTERN.

INSTRUCTIONS FOR MAKING PICKET STITCH.

Make a pattern from the engraving and stamp the design upon the material.

Bring the needle up from underneath through dot 1, (see above diagram,) thrust it down through dot 2, bring it up through dot 3, thrust it down through dot 4, bring it up through dot 5, thrust it down through dot 6, bring it up through dot 7, thrust it down through dot 8, bring it up through dot 9, thrust it down through dot 10, bring it up through dot 11, thrust it down through dot 12, bring it up through dot 13, thrust it down through dot 14, bring it up through dot 15, thrust it down through dot 16, bring it up through dot 17, thrust it down through dot 18, bring it up through dot 19, thrust it down through dot 20. You now bind the pickets together (which should be done with a different color of thread from that used for making the pickets in order to give the work a more beautiful effect,) bring the needle up from underneath through dot A, thrust it down through dot B, bring it up through dot C, thrust it down through dot D, bring it up through dot E, thrust it down through dot F, bring it up through dot G, thrust it down through dot H, bring it up through dot J, thrust it down through dot K, bring it up through dot L, thrust it down through dot M, bring it up through dot N, thrust it down through dot P, bring it up through dot H, thrust it down through dot Q. You have now completed two pannels continue in like manner until your work is finished.

This is one of the most popular and effective of all stitches represented in art needle work and is suitable for a wide range of work with embroidery silks, zephyrs, flosses and crewels.

CHAIN STITCH DIAGRAM AND PATTERN.

INSTRUCTIONS FOR MAKING CHAIN STITCH.

To make this stitch, first lay out the work by placing dots upon the material where the chain is wanted, as shown by the above pattern. Hold the material so that the needle will point towards your left in working.

Bring the needle up from underneath through dot 1, (see above diagram,) pulling the thread all the way through. Insert it just back of where it was brought up and bring the point out in dot 2, loop the thread over the point of the needle, place the thumb of the left hand firmly over the loop so as to hold it in place while you draw the thread all the way through; (this operation makes one link) then insert the needle just inside of the link already made and bring the point out in dot 3, loop the thread over the point of the needle and draw it all the way through as before and continue the operation in like manner until the chain is finished.

This simple yet very effective stitch may be used for embroidering mats for fastening down the edges of applique work and for outlining, or it may follow the edge of a cord conched on fancy work.

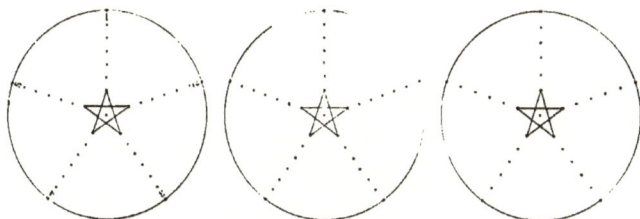

Star Stitch Diagram and Pattern

INSTRUCTIONS FOR MAKING STAR STITCH.

Make a pattern from the engraving and stamp the design upon the material. (In making the pattern it is not necessary to stamp the circle lines seen in the engraving simply the dots.) Commence at the point of the star and work toward the centre, numbering the dots in each line from the extreme points to the centre of the same; bring the needle up from underneath through dot 1 of the first line, (see above diagram,) thrust it down through dot 1 of the third line, bring it up through dot 1 of the fourth line, thrust it down through dot 1 of the second line, bring it up through dot 1 of the fifth line, thrust it down through dot 1 of the second line, bring it up through dot 1 of the third line, thrust it down through dot 1 of the fifth line, bring it up through dot 1 of the fourth line, thrust it down through dot 1 of the first line, you have now formed a star; continue as follows: Bring the needle up through dot 2 of the first line, thrust it down through dot 2 of the third line, bring it up through dot 2 of the fourth line, thrust it down through dot 2 of the second line, bring it up through dot 2 of the fifth line, thrust it down through dot 2 of the second line, bring it up through dot 2 of the third line, thrust it down through dot 2 of the fifth line, bring it up throught dot 2 of the fourth line, thrust it down through dot 2 of the first line and continue in like manner until the star is finished.

The stars may be worked in red, white and blue or one may be worked in red, one in white and one in blue to represent our National colors.

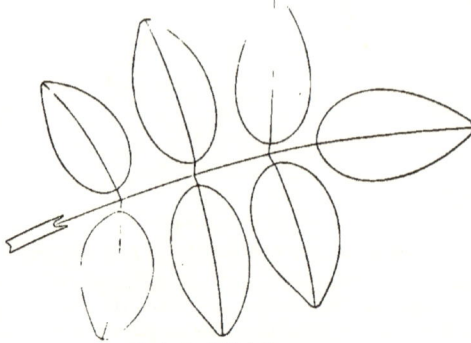

Eureka Leaf Stitch Pattern

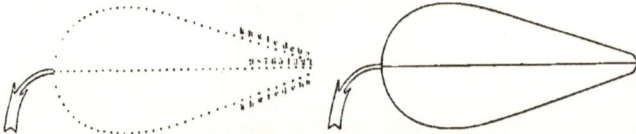

Eureka Stitch Diagram and Leaf Pattern

INSTRUCTIONS FOR MAKING EUREKA STITCH.

Make a pattern from the leaf engraving and stamp the design upon the material. Hold the material so that the point of the leaf will be to the right in working. Commence by working the lower part of the leaf first by bringing the needle up from underneath through dot A, (see above diagram,) thrust it down through dot 1, bring it up through dot 2, thrust it down through dot B, bring it up through dot C, thrust it down through dot 3, bring it up through dot 4, thrust it down through dot D, bring it up through dot E, thrust it down through dot 5, bring it up through dot 6, thrust it down through dot F, bring it up through dot G, thrust it down through dot 7, bring it up through dot 8, thrust it down through dot H, bring it up through dot K, thrust it down through dot 9, and continue the operation in like manner until the lower half of the leaf is finished. To make the upper half of the leaf, bring the needle up from underneath through dot A, thrust it down through dot 1, bring it up through dot 2, thrust it down through dot B, bring it up through dot C, thrust it down through dot 3, bring it up through dot 4, thrust it down through dot D, bring it up through dot E, thrust it down through dot 5, bring it up through dot 6, thrust it down through dot F, bring it up through dot G, thrust it down through dot 7, bring it up through dot 8, thrust it down through dot H, bring it up through dot K, thrust it down through dot 9 and continue the operation in like manner until the leaf is finished. A leaf worked in this stitch can be shaded and may be either green or in brilliant colors to represent the tintings which autumn gives them, and is suitable for toilet articles and for table covers or for any article where a surface stitch is required. The stems of the leaves are made with the stem stitch. After having learned to make this leaf, you should take the stitches closer together than those represented in the above dotted diagram so that the thread will neatly cover the material between the outlines.

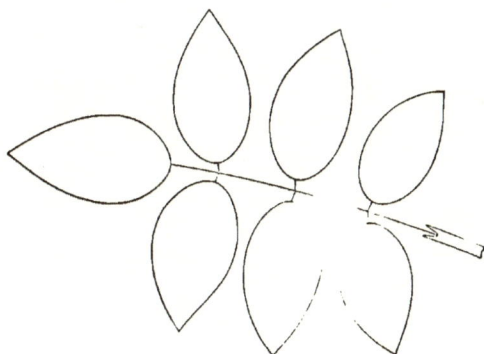

Janina Leaf Stitch Pattern

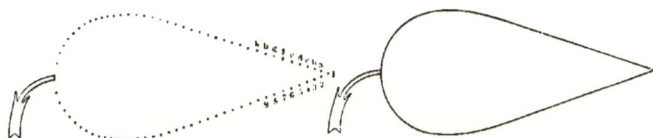

Janina Stitch Diagram and Leaf Pattern

INSTRUCTIONS FOR MAKING JANINA STITCH.

Make a pattern from the leaf engraving and stamp the design upon the material. Hold the material so that the point of the leaf will be to your right in working and bring the needle up from underneath through dot 4,(see above diagram,) insert it in dot 1, bring it out in dot C, insert it in dot 2, bring it out in dot 5, insert it in dot A bring it out in dot D, insert it in dot 3, bring it out in dot G, insert it in dot B, bring it out in dot E, insert it half way between dots 4 and 5, bring it out in dot 7, insert it half way between dots C and D, bring it out in dot F, insert it half way between dots 5 and G, bring it out in dot 8, insert it half way between dots D and E, bring it out in dot G, insert it half way between dots 6 and 7, bring it out in dot 9, insert it half way between dots E and F, bring it out in dot H, and continue the operation in like manner by always inserting the needle to the right, half way between the second and third last stitches, bringing the point out to the left the length of one stitch until the leaf is finished. This stitch, like the Eureka stitch, is suitable for toilet articles and for table covers or for any article where a surface stitch is required. The stems of the leaves are made with the stem stitch. After having learned to make this leaf you should take the stitches closer together than those represented in the above dotted diagram, so that the thread will neatly cover the material between the outlines.

Japan Cockscomb Pattern

INSTRUCTIONS FOR MAKING JAPAN COCKSCOMB DESIGN.

Make a pattern from the engraving and stamp the design upon the material.

The entire flower and the stem is made with the plush stitch by using three or four shades of garnet filloselle. Begin by filling in all such parts as are marked A, B, and C, (as shown in the engraving,) with large French knots of a light shade of Berlin wool, make the knots quite large and close, then fill in the remainder of the comb with darker knots, making them smaller as you get near the edge. This done, commence filling in the filloselle in the darkest shade and when you come to any of the parts such as those marked A, B, and C, fill them in with lighter shades. The filling in should be worked close and left quite long. The lower part from C, down to the point where the leaf crosses the stem, shows the green seeds with a thin sprinkling of velvety down. This is imitated by making the knots of grayish green crewel, filling it in with a strand of filloselle made by mixing in a few threads of the light garnet with the grayish green filloselle, having less garnet as you get near the leaf. The remainder of the stem is filled in with pure gray-green filloselle clipped quite closely. The leaf is stitched on in four shades of olive arrasene twisted. Begin by making the large vein with the darkest shade with the stem stitch, next put in the other veins with the next darkest shade, now take your lighter shade and stitch on the upper part of the leaf in a sort of outline stitch, beginning at the point where the leaf touches the stem of the cockscomb, stitch on the lower side of the leaf in the same way and about the same distance from the point, slanting the arrasene in the direction indicated by the veins seen in the engraving of the leaf, outline the remainder of the leaf with the next lighter shade, now fill in the remainder of the leaf with a shade a trifle lighter than that used for the veins, blending as well as you can. This flower is very effective when made up into a wall banner on felt or plush, and can be used for a great variety of decorative articles.

INSTRUCTIONS FOR MAKING PLUSH STITCH.

The flower to be made is first filled in with the French knot stitch, to furnish a foundation and a number of strands of floss are tied with a single thread into bunches the desired thickness, of about one-half inch in length, clip the bunches off, bring the needle up from underneath through the design between the knots and place a bunch over the knots close to it and thrust the needle back through the design on the opposite side of the bunch, near where it came up. Continue the operation in this manner until your work is finished. The ends of the floss after being sewed down between the knot should be clipped off evenly with a sharp pair of scissors and this should be done after the filling in is completed.

This stitch is used for making Japan Cockscomb, Princes Feather, Tops of Rushes and Sumach. Only flowers similar in their nature to those described, can be worked in this manner.

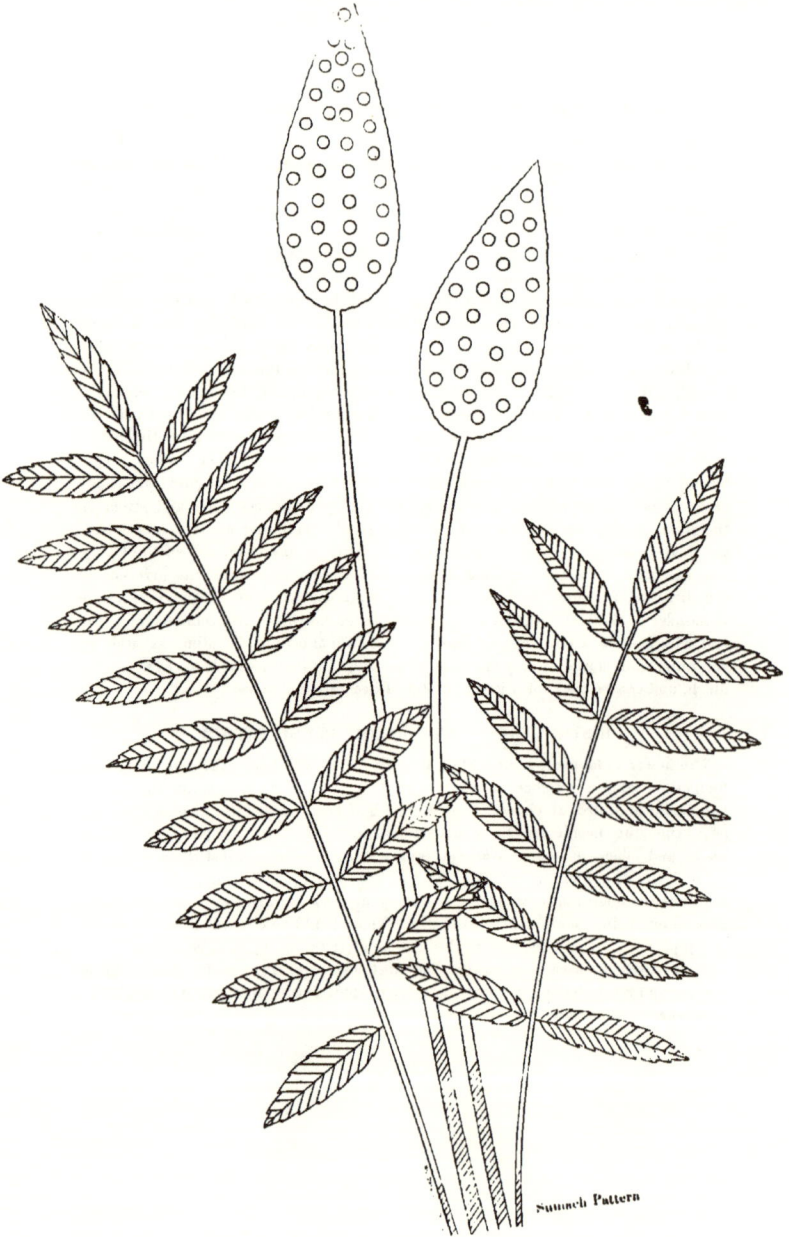

Sumach Pattern

INSTRUCTIONS FOR MAKING SUMACH DESIGN.

Make a pattern from the engraving and stamp the design upon the material.

The stems are made with dark green etching or embroidery silk in the satin stitch the leaves with dark green arrasene, the foundation for the tops are made with red Berlin wool or common yarn in the French knot stitch and are finished with dark red filloselle. Work all the stems first; commence at the bottom and work toward the top, giving the stitches the slant indicated by the cross lines seen in the engraving of the stem. To make the leaves, thread a needle with silk to match the arrasene in color and stitch on one-half of the leaf first and then the other, beginning where the leaf joins the stem, stitching on the arrasene back and forth from the central vein of the leaf to the outside edge in both cases, giving the arrasene the slant indicated by the lines seen in the engraving of the leaves; now fill in the tops with large French knots as indicated by the dots seen in the engraving of the tops, (this furnished a foundation for the dark red filloselle,) thread a needle with button-hole twist to match the filloselle in color and stitch on the filloselle over the knots with the plush stitch and lastly with a sharp pair of scissors trim off the ends of the filloselle round and evenly and your work is completed.

INSTRUCTIONS FOR MAKING PERFORATED PATTERNS.

Place tracing paper over the engraved design and with a lead pencil trace the outlines with a steady hand. The design being accurately traced, the pattern is ready to be perforated. Lay a couple of folds of cloth on the table, place the traced pencil sketch upon this and with a needle of the medium size prick out the pattern, being very careful to follow the outlines and make the perforations quite close, (or you can perforate the outlines to good advantage on a sewing machine by removing the thread from the needle.) By placing three or four sheets of paper under the traced sketch and pinning them together, a number of patterns can be perforated at once.

INSTRUCTIONS FOR MAKING STAMPING POWDER.

Take six parts powdered rosin and four parts Marine or Prussian blue, (best quality,) mix well together.

INSTRUCTIONS FOR MAKING INDELIBLE STAMPING PAINT.

First get a small can of best zinc white, ground in oil, (in case you cannot get zinc white, white lead ground in oil will answer almost as well.) Put a small portion of it in a saucer and mix it with boiled linseed oil to about the thickness of cream it is then ready for use. A little turpentine or japan dryer may be added to the paint to assist it to dry, but if too much is added it will cause the pain to dry on the pattern before you can get time to clean it.

INSTRUCTIONS FOR MAKING BLACK LIQUID STAMPING FLUID.

It is made by putting a very little lamp black into a bottle containing benzine. Put in just enough to make it a pale black when shaken. This makes an excellent stamping liquid as it dries as soon as applied and will not rub off and the patterns need no cleaning after they are used. It must be kept securely corked to prevent evaporation and away from the fire.

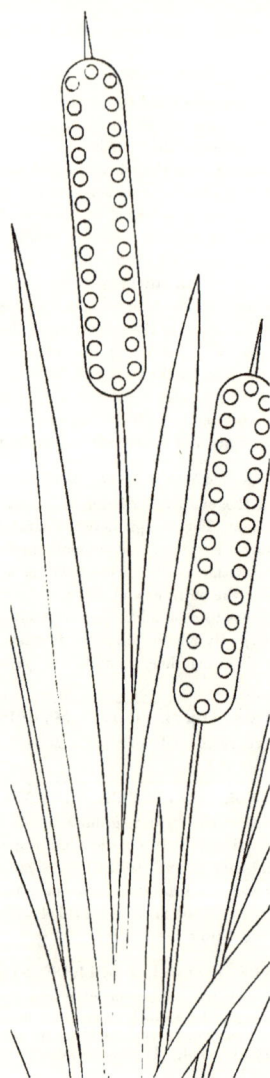

INSTRUCTIONS FOR MAKING RUSH DESIGN.

Make a pattern from the engraving and stamp the design upon the material. The stems and blades are made with bright olive green etching silk, with the satin stitch begin at the bottom of the stem and work toward the top, giving the stitches the slant indicated by the lines seen in the engraving of the stem. To make the blades commence at the point where the blade joins the stem and work to the point of the blade, giving the stitches the slant indicated by the lines seen in the engraving of the blades. To make the tops, begin by filling in two rows of large French knots through the centre as shown by the dots in the engraving of the tops, using brown Berlin wool or common yarn for that purpose, this forms a foundation for the brown filloselle. The tops are filled in with the plush stitch, using brown filloselle for filling and brown button-hole twist for stitching on the filloselle; the points that project from the tops of the rushes seen in the engraving are made with the stem stitch, or they may be made in the satin stitch, and should be a trifle lighter in color than that used for the stems. Now with a sharp pair of scissors trim off the ends of the filloselle round and evenly and your work is ready to be made up into a banner or any article that fancy may suggest.

INSTRUCTIONS FOR MAKING POUNCET.

A good pouncet is made by tacking a piece of chamois leather to the smooth side of a block of wood two inches square and one inch thick, or take a strip of fine felt about an inch wide, (a strip from an old felt hat is as good as anything,) roll it up tightly into a roll and wrap it securely with cord, leaving the end flat and rub the end over a piece of sand paper to make it smooth and even.

INSTRUCTIONS FOR STAMPING WITH POWDER.

Stamping should be done on a smooth table covered with two or three thicknesses of cotton or ticking, upon this lay the material to be stamped, then lay the pattern on rough side up secure it in position by placing heavy weights upon one end or side of it, hold the other side or end of the pattern with one hand and apply the powder with the other. Take a small portion of the powder on the pouncet and rub it first on some smooth surface, then strike it sharply against some hard surface to remove any surplus powder that may be upon it, then rub it over the pattern, back and forth with a moderate pressure, being careful not to let the pattern slip and cause the lines to blur. Take more powder as is found necessary. The unsecured end or side of the pattern may be raised from time to time to allow you to see how the work is progressing. It will drop back into place again. Then remove the pattern carefully and lay a piece of thin paper over the stamping and pass a hot iron over it, this melts the gum in the powder and fastens the pattern to the material. The iron should be as hot as possible without scorching the cloth. Should the heat change the color of the material, iron it all over. Should the perforations become clogged or filled up they are easily cleaned by laying them flat on the table and rubbing both sides with a soft woolen cloth..

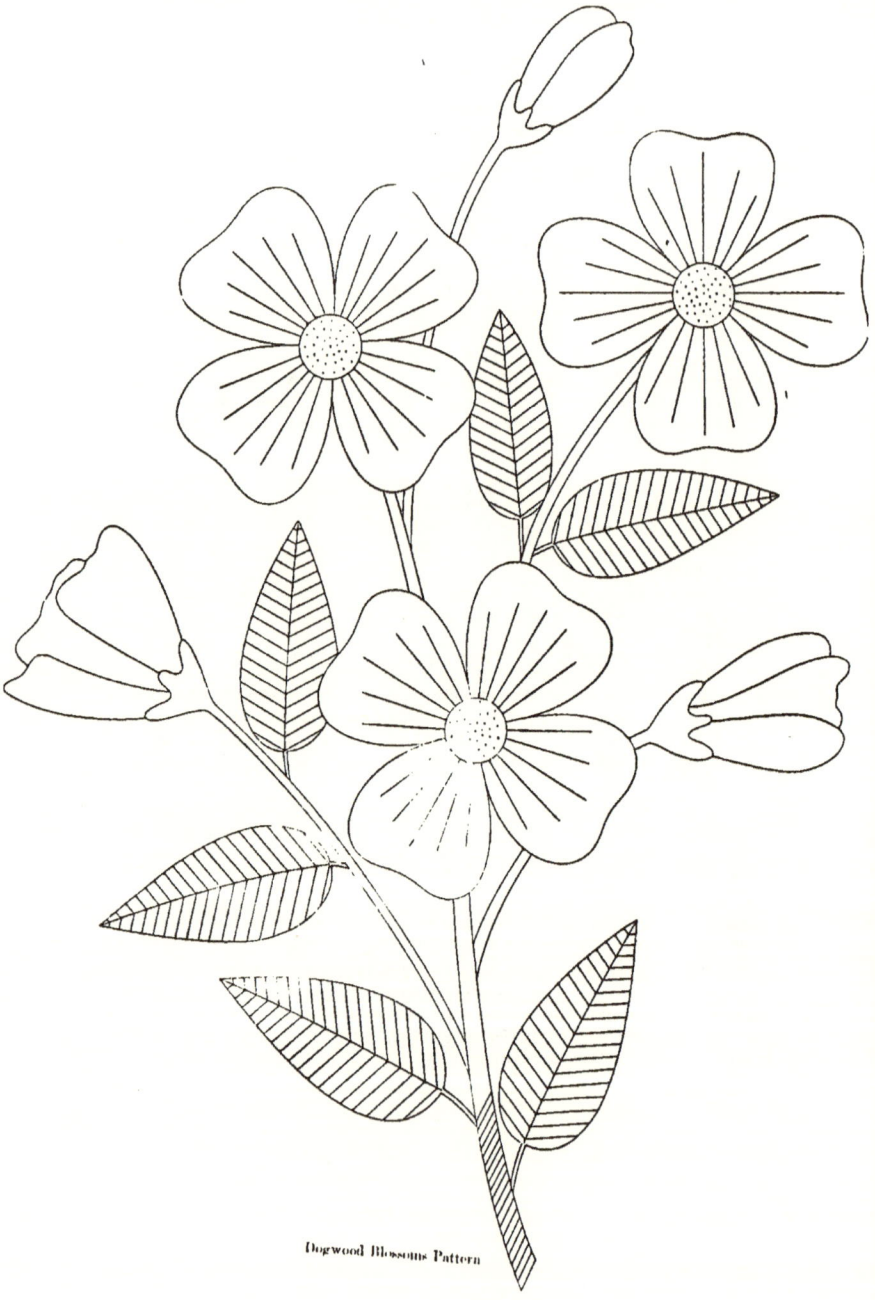

Dogwood Blossoms Pattern

INSTRUCTIONS FOR MAKING DOGWOOD BLOSSOM DESIGN IN VELVET.

Make a pattern from the engraving and stamp the design upon the material. The stems are made with olive-green etching silk in the satin stitch. Commence working the stems at the bottom and work towards the top of the spray, giving the stitches the slant indicated by the lines seen in the engraving of the stem. The leaves are made in three shades of green arrasene, select shades that partake of a yellowish-green cast and as you near the top of the spray use more of the lighter shades. Thread a needle with silk to match the arrasene in color and stitch on one-half of the leaf first and then the other, beginning where the leaf joins the stem, stitching on the arrasene back and forth from the central vein of the leaf to the outside edge in both cases, giving the arrasene the slant indicated by the cross lines seen in the engraving of the leaves. The veins seen in the engraving of the leaf are put in after the leaves are finished, using a dark shade of embroidery floss or veining chenile. The flowers are cut out of creamy white molskin velvet, cut cardboard the exact shape and a fraction smaller than the outlined petal indicated by the flower seen in the engraving, cut the velvet large enough so that it will neatly cover over and tuck under the cardboard, gather the edges of the velvet together with needle and thread tightly, so that the upper surface will lay flat and smooth, then fasten the petals upon the material with a single thread of bright yellow floss, taking the stitches from the small circle in the centre of the petals to near the edge of the same as indicated by the vein lines seen in the engraving of the flower. To make the buds cut out a piece of velvet to match the petals in color, about two inches square, gather it through the centre and cover the gathering with arrasene in such a way as to give the bud the appearance of peeping out from under, using the same shade of arrasene for the covering of the bud as that used for making the leaves. The centre of the flowers are filled in with large French knots, as indicated by the dots seen in the centre of the engraving of the flower, using dark yellow embroidery floss having some knots made of seal brown floss. Work all the stems first, then the leaves and buds before fastening on the petals and lastly the French knots in the centre.

INSTRUCTIONS FOR STAMPING WITH PAINT.

Place the pattern on the cloth, smooth side up, though either side will work well weight the pattern down as in stamping with powder and pouncet, spread a little of the paint in a row along the edge of the pattern farthest from you, then draw it over the perforations of the pattern with a rather limber table knife. The paint must not be allowed to dry on the pattern, but both sides must be immediately cleaned with benzine or gasoline and a soft cloth. Sprinkle or pour it over the pattern then rub dry with a cloth. There is not the least danger of its injuring the pattern.

Wheat Pattern

INSTRUCTIONS FOR MAKING WHEAT DESIGN.

Make a pattern from the engraving and stamp the design upon the material. The stems, grains and barbs are made with old gold colored etching silk or fillo-selle and the blades with a very light olive-green etching silk, the stems are made in the satin stitch, or they may be made in the stem stitch, work all the stems first, commence at the bottom and work toward the top, giving the stitches the slant in-dicated by the cross lines seen in the engraving of the stem, then work the blades in the satin stitch, beginning where the blade joins the stem and work toward the point, giving the stitches the slant indicated by the cross lines seen in the engraving of the blade, now make the grains in the wheat grain stitch, begin at the bottom of the head and work alternatly on either side to the top or point of the head, then work the centre grains, working from the top to the bottom of the head and which are made without barbs except the centre grain at the extreme point of the head as indicated by the engraving, lastly make the barbs, (the small delicate thread-like fibre that projects from the point of the grain as indicated by the engraving of the head,) which must be made with a much finer thread than that used for making the grains, in order to give the design the desired effect.

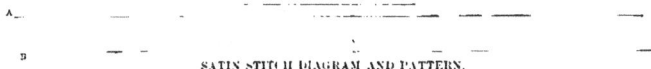

A

B

SATIN STITCH DIAGRAM AND PATTERN.

INSTRUCTIONS FOR MAKING SATIN STITCH.

Draw upon the material where you desire to make the stitch, two parallel lines of equal length and of about one-fourth of an inch apart as indicated by the above out-line engraving or of whatever width you desire to make the stitch. The right-hand outline B should extend beyond the left hand outline A, equal to one-half the distance the lines are placed apart, in order to give the stitches the proper slant as indicated by the above outlined engraving. In working this stitch, great care must be taken that the edges are worked even on both sides and the stitches taken very close so that the thread will neatly cover the space between the outlines of the pattern. Hold the material so that in working, the needle will point to the left and work from you. Bring the needle up from underneath through the end of outline A, (see above diagram,) insert the needle in the end of outline B, bring it out in out-line A, insert the needle in outline B, bring it out in outline A, and continue the operation in like manner by always inserting the needle in outline B, and bringing it out in outline A until your work is completed. This stitch is used for making the stems of the following flowers: Dogwood, Fuchsia, Golden Rod, Poppy, Plush Rose, Rushes, Scotch Thistle, Sumach, Wheat and for making the blades of Rushes, blades of Wheat, etc.

INSTRUCTIONS FOR STAMPING WITH LIQUID FLUID.

Take an empty spool, plug up the hole with wood and make a distributor by fold-ing two or three ply of felt over one end, leaving the felt long enough to overlap part of the side of the spool, securing the felt to the spool by winding it with twine. You now place the felt end of the spool to the mouth of the bottle and tip it up a number of times until the distributor is well saturated, now place the perforated pattern upon the material to be stamped, smooth side up, and rub the saturated distributor over the perforations.

Golden Rod Pattern   For-get-me-not
Pattern

INSTRUCTIONS FOR MAKING GOLDEN ROD DESIGN.

Make a pattern from the engraving and stamp the design upon the material.

The stems are worked with dark green etching silk in the stem stitch, or they may be worked in the satin stitch. Make the large stem first then the smaller ones, working them the full length of the branches as shown in the engraving. The leaves are worked in the eureka or janina stitch, using the same shade of etching silk as that used for making the stems, or they may be made of dark-green arrasene as follows: Thread a needle with silk to match the arrasene in color and stitch on one-half of the leaf first and then the other, beginning where the leaf joins the stem, stitching on the arrasene back and forth from the centre of the leaf to the outside edge, in both cases giving the arrasene the slant indicated by the lines seen in the leaves of the engraving, now fill in the branches with French knots, using yellow filloselle in its pure golden hues. The knots and filling in stitches must be done with neatness, but regularity in arrangement need not be aimed at as they may be taken up whenever there is a necessity.

INSTRUCTIONS FOR MAKING FORGET-ME-NOT DESIGN.

Make a pattern from the engraving and stamp the design upon the material.

The stems and leaves are worked with green silk floss, the flowers and buds with blue filloselle and the centres of the flowers with old gold or yellow colored silk floss. Work all the stems first, commencing at the bottom and work each of them the full length of the branches. The stems are worked in the stem stitch, the leaves in the eureka or janina stitch, the flowers and buds in the forget-me-not stitch or they may be made in the wheat grain stitch. The centre of the flower is filled in with the French knot stitch. After having finished the stems, work the leaves, then the flowers and buds, lastly fill in the centre of the flowers.

INSTRUCTIONS FOR MAKING FRENCH KNOT STITCH.

To make this stitch bring the needle up from underneath at the point where the knot is wanted, now catch the thread with the left hand about two inches from the material upon which you work, hold the needle in the right hand quite close to the material and with the left hand wind the thread twice or thrice around the point of the needle, after which hold the thread tightly and with the fore-finger of the right hand, shove the wound thread down towards the point of the needle as you thrust it back through the material at about the same place it was brought up. This operation forms the knot; you then bring the needle up where the next knot is wanted and repeat the operation. This stitch is used for the foundation of the blossoms of the Scotch Thistle, Tops of Rushes, Sumach, Japan Cockscomb, Plush Stitch and is used in making Golden Rod, Ends of Stamens and the Centre of Flowers.

Plush Rose Pattern

INSTRUCTIONS FOR MAKING PLUSH ROSE DESIGN.

Make a pattern from the engraving and stamp the design upon the material.

The stems are made with olive-green etching or embroidery silk in the satin stitch, or they may be made with olive-green chenille, work all the stems first commence at the bottom and work toward the top giving the stitches the slant indicated by the lines seen in the engraving of the stem. The leaves are made with olive-green chenille, thread a needle with silk to match the chenille in color and stitch on one-half of the leaf first and then the other, beginning where the leaf joins the stem stitching on the chenille back and forth from the central vein of the leaf to the outside edge in both cases, giving the chenille the slant indicated by the lines seen in the engraving of the leaves. The roses are made by cutting silk into small squares, (care being taken to select a shade appropriate to the rose,) doubling each of them on the bias, thus forming triangles and then bringing the three corners together by gathering, this forms a petal of which five are then made. A piece of buckram is then cut the exact shape and size of the outline of the rose seen in the engraving upon which the petals are sewed, this is begun at the circumference and the centre is filled in with smaller petals. To make a bud, a large petal is used, it is gathered through the centre and the gathering covered with chenille in such a way as to give the bud the appearance of peeping out from under, the centre of the rose, is filled in with French knots as shown by the dots inclosed within the circle seen in the engraving of the rose, care being taken that the color of floss used for the knots is appropriate to the rose, the vein lines seen in the centre of the engraving of the petals, running from the centre circle to near the outer edge of the petals are made with a single strand of floss, using the same shade as that used for the knots.

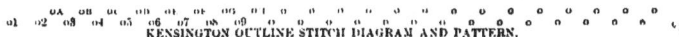

KENSINGTON OUTLINE STITCH DIAGRAM AND PATTERN.

INSTRUCTIONS FOR MAKING KENSINGTON OUTLINE STITCH.

Make a pattern from the engraving and stamp the design upon the material.

Hold the material so that the needle will point to the left and allow the thread to drop from you in working. Bring the needle up from underneath through dot 1, (see above diagram,) insert it in dot A, bring the point out in dot 2, insert it in dot B, bring the point out in dot 3, insert it in dot C, bring the point out in dot 4, insert it in dot D, bring the point out in dot 5, insert it in dot E, bring the point out in dot 6, insert it in dot F, bring the point out in dot 7, insert it in dot G, bring the point out in dot 8, insert it in dot H, bring the point out in dot 9 and continue the operation by inserting the needle in the upper right hand dot and bringing the point out in the lower left hand dot until your work is finished.

This stitch is in reality the same as the stem stitch, only that by the insertion now and then of a stroke representing the folds of drapery and the veins of leaves, the unbroken outline is relieved. This is now recognized as the best stitch for embroidery work. The favorite designs for this stitch are foliage, butterflies, and animals and they are usually made on satin. This stitch represents outline sketching with a pencil or crayon.

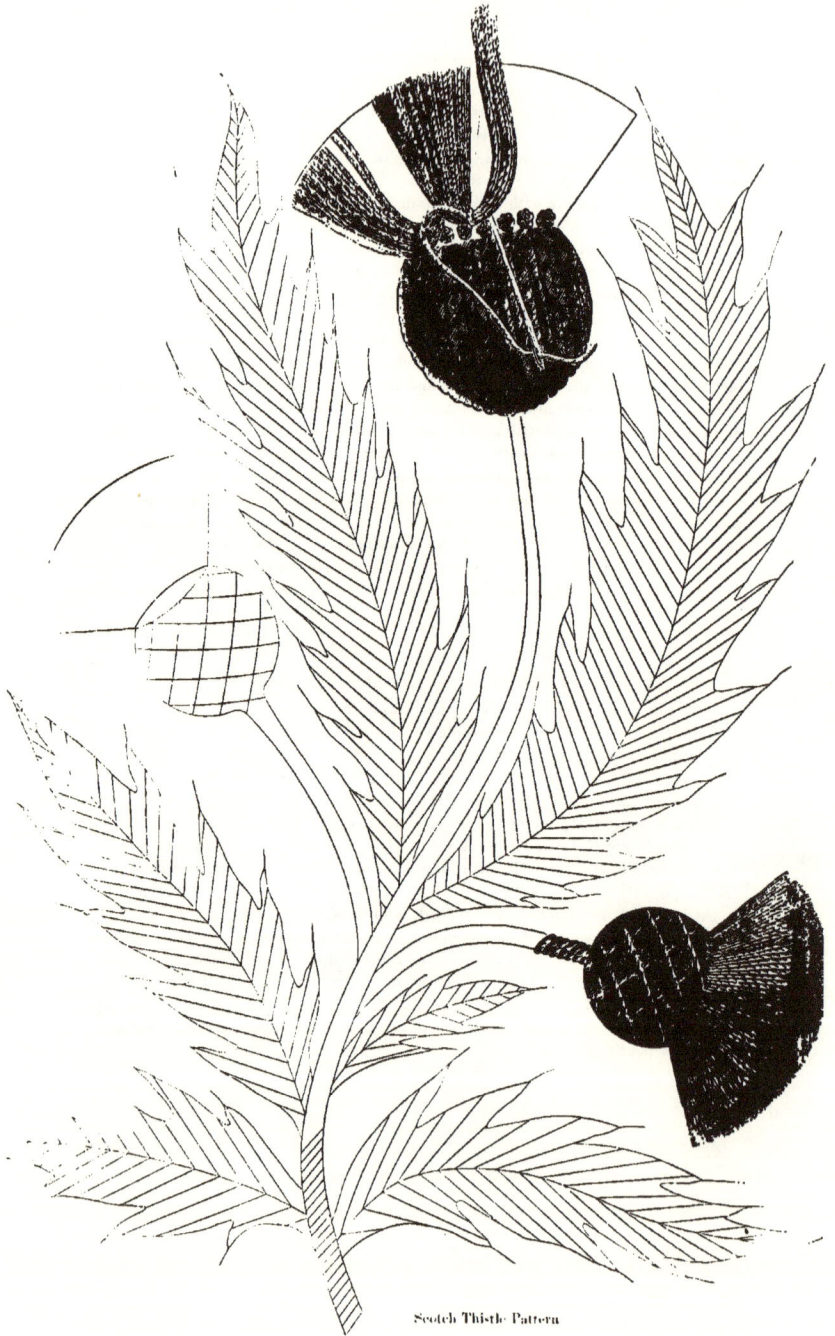

Scotch Thistle Pattern

INSTRUCTIONS FOR MAKING SCOTCH THISTLE DESIGN.

Make a pattern from the engraving and stamp the design upon the material. Commence by working the stems first with the satin stitch beginning at the bottom of the large stem, giving the stitches the slant indicated by the lines seen in the engraving of the large stem, then the smaller ones giving the stitches the same slant using olive-green embroidery or etching silk for that purpose. Now fill in three rows of large French knots, four knots in each row and one in each corner of the the oblong circle seen just above the bulb in the outlined blossom on the left hand side in the engraving, using common yarn for that purpose. This furnishes a foundation for the mauve filloselle, (a thistle pink) this done, fill in each bulb with a gray shade of Berlin wool or common yarn as shown in the engraving of the partly finished blossom, stitch the yarn on with needle and thread, back and forth, then cross-wise until you give the bulb a natural rounded appearance. The mauve filloselle to form the blossom should be doubled to about the thickness of a small size lead pencil lay the end of the filloselle about one and a half inches above the upper row of knots, looping it around the knots as you lay it back and forth. Thread a needle with strong thread and bring it up from underneath between the upper row of knots catching the filloselle as the needle is passed back through the material, drawing the thread tightly, this has a tendency to make the filloselle stand out straight and as you do not want this effect for the blossom you at once see that something more is needed to make the filloselle lay flat on the material, hence we take another fastening stitch as shown in the pattern, and catch both strands of the filloselle a little above the last stitch which causes the filloselle to lay flat and this operation is repeated until three rows of filloselle are sewed down, a glance at the finished blossom shown in the pattern will give an idea of the effect to be aimed at. The leaves are made with a grayish-green arrasene, thread a needle with silk to match the arrasene in color and stitch on one-half of the leaf first and then the other, beginning in the center of the leaf where it joins the stem, stitching on the arrasene back and forth from the center to the outside edge in both cases or you may make the leaf by stitching on the arrasene back and forth from one edge of the leaf to the other, giving the arrasene in both cases the slant indicated by the lines seen in the engraving of the leaves, and with the same thread make short stitches here and there to represent the thorns on the edge of the leaves as indicated by the short lines seen projecting from the edge of the leaves seen in the engraving. By working in this manner no arrasene is wasted on the underside of the material. The leaves being stitched on and the upper part of the blossom being filled in with filloselle, now begin to cover the yarn foundation of each bulb with the same shade of arrasene as that used for the leaves, stitching on the arrasene diagonally over the bulb, stitch the arrasene quite close so that none of the yarn foundation will show through, stitch the arrasene up so as to join the filloselle which forms the blossom. now thread a needle with olive-green etching silk and carry long stitches back and forth over the arrasene in such a way as to form squares on the bulb. Now comb out the blossoms to give them a downy appearance, the ends of the filloselle is then clipped with a sharp pair of scissors, the shape indicated by the circle lines seen above the bulbs and your work is ready to be made up into any article that fancy might suggest.

FEATHER STITCH DIAGRAM AND PATTERN.
INSTRUCTIONS FOR MAKING FEATHER STITCH.

To make this stitch, draw upon the material where you desire to make the stitch, three parallel lines of equal length, three-eighths of an inch apart as indicated by the above outlined engraving, or of whatever width you desire to make the stitch. The centre line B, should extend beyond the two outside lines A and C, equal to one-half the distance that A and C are placed apart in order to give the stitches the proper slant as indicated by the above outlined engraving. In working this stitch, great care must be taken that the edges of the feather is worked even on both sides and the stitches taken very close so that the thread will neatly cover the spaces between the outlines of the pattern, (the centre or stem of the feather is made with the stem stitch after the sides are finished.) Hold the material so that in working the feather will point from you. Bring the needle up from underneath through the end of outline A, (see above diagram,) take a stitch in the end of outline B, thrust the needle down and bring it up in the end of outline C, take a stitch in outline B, thrust the needle down and bring it up in outline A, take a stitch in outline B, thrust the needle down and bring it up in outline C, and continue the operation in this manner until your work is completed. This stitch can be worked to good advantage in the following manner: Hold the material so that in working the point of the feather will be to your right. Bring the needle up from underneath through the end of outline A, take a stitch in the end of outline B, pointing the needle to the right take a stitch in the end of outline C, pointing the needle to the left take a stitch in outline B, pointing the needle to the left take a stitch in outline A, pointing the needle to the left take a stitch in outline B, pointing the needle to the right you will observe that the needle is pointed to the left at all times except when working down from outline A toward outline C, the needle is pointed to the right in outline B. This stitch when worked in two colors, produces a very pretty effect.

BLANKET OR BUTTON-HOLE STITCH DIAGRAM AND PATTERN.
INSTRUCTIONS FOR MAKING BLANKET OR BUTTON HOLE STITCH.

Draw upon the material where you desire to make the stitch, two parallel lines of equal length and of about one-fourth of an an inch apart as indicated by the above outline engraving or of whatever width you desire to make the stitch. In working this stitch great care must be taken that the edges are worked even on both sides and the stitches taken very close so that the the thread will neatly cover the space between the outlines of the pattern. Hold the material so that in working the needle will point to the left and work from you. Bring the needle up from underneath through the end of outline A, (see above diagram,) insert the needle in the end of outline B, bring the point out in outline A, loop the thread over the needle and place the thumb of the left hand firmly over the loop so as to hold it in place until you draw the thread all the way through, insert the needle in outline B, bring the point out in outline A, loop the thread over the needle, place the thumb of the left hand over the loop and draw the thread all the way through and continue the operation in like manner by always inserting the needle in outline B and bringing the point out in outline A, looping the thread over the needle and placing the thumb of the left hand over the loop and drawing the thread all the way through as before until your work is completed.

INSTRUCTIONS FOR MAKING DOG-WOOD BLOSSOM DESIGN IN ARRASENE.

Make a pattern from the engraving on page 22 and stamp the design upon the material.

The stems are made with olive-green etching silk in the satin stitch. Commence working the stems at the bottom and work towards the top of the spray, giving the stitches the slant indicated by the lines seen in the engraving of the stems. The leaves are made in three shades of green arrasene, select shades that partake of a yellowish green cast, and as you near the top of the spray use more of the lighter shades. Thread a needle with silk to match the arrasene in color and stitch on one half of the leaf first and then the other, beginning where the leaf joins the stem stitching on the arrasene back and forth from the central vein of the leaf to the outside edge in both cases, giving the layers of arrasene the slant indicated by the lines seen in the engraving of the leaves.

The sepals that show on the back of some of the blossoms and buds are also made of green arrasene and are stitched on the same as the leaves. The veins are put in the leaves and sepals after they have been stitched on, with a very dark shade of embroidery floss or veining chenille. The petals may be made in two shades of cream white arrasene or in two shades of white ribbosene, using the darker shade near the centre. Begin by stitching on the arrasene, (using white silk thread for that purpose,) back and forth from the outer edge of the circle seen in the engraving of the flower to the outside edge of the petal, being very careful to keep the ends of the arrasene which are near the centre of the flower closer together than the ends nearer the outside edge, so that the petal will converge towards the centre.

The centres of the flowers are filled in with large French knots, using dark yellow embroidery floss, having some knots made of seal brown floss.

The veins in the petals as shown in the engraving are put in with one long stitch for each vein using a light shade of yellow floss.

If the work presents a drawn appearance when finished, this can be remedied by steaming the back of it and then stretching it over a board for a short time.

This graceful design of dog wood blossoms is well adapted to the greatest variety of decorative purposes, bracket drapes, wall banners, sofa cushions, and chair tidies.

INSTRUCTIONS FOR MAKING FUCHSIA DESIGN.

The stems are worked with dark green etching silk in the satin stitch. The leaves are made in three shades of dark green arrasene. The flowers may be made in the same mauve tints, using two shades of mauve arrasene, or the flowers on one branch may be made in delicate pink tints using two or three shades of pink arrasene. The parts shown light in the fuchsia are made with white arrasene. Work all the stems first, commencing at the bottom and working toward the top of the spray, giving the stitches the slant indicated by the dotted lines seen in the pattern of the stem. To make the leaves, use the darkest of the three shades of arrasene for the lower leaves and the lighter shades as you approach the top of the spray varying the shades in each leaf. Thread a needle with silk to match the arrasene in color and stitch on one-half of the leaf first, and then the other, begining where the leaf joins the stem, stitching on the arrasene back and forth from the central vein of the leaf to the outside edge in both cases, giving the layers of arrasene the slant indicated by the dotted lines seen in the pattern of the leaf, proceed to make the other half of the leaf as well as all others in the same way. To make the flowers fill in a small portion of light mauve arrasene near the white portion then work in the darker shades last, blending the shades into each other vary the shading in each flower. If it be desired to make the flowers on one branch in pink tints it can be done in the same way by using two or three shades of pink arrasene. The buds are made with white arrasene, having a very light pale green blended in near the bulb, (that part nearest the stem.) To make the bulb, thread a needle with any ordinary sewing thread and stitch on Berlin wool or common yarn, back and forth, then crosswise, double the yarn and repeat the stitches until you give the bulb a natural rounded appearance; now cover this yarn foundation with a medium shade of green arrasene, stitching on the arrasene diagonally over the bulb, stitch the arrasene quite closely so that none of the yarn foundation will show through, stitch the arrasene up so as to join the arrasene which forms the blossom. The anthers are put in with the French knot stitch at the end of each stamen, using a bright pink etching silk to make the knots. The stamens (thread-like organs protruding from the point of the flowers) are put in with bright colored etching silk. The veins of the leaves are put in as follows: Thread a needle with dark green embroidery floss and bring it up from underneath through the material at the upper end of the central vein now draw the floss down to the point where the first cross vein meets the central one, hold the floss into place with the thumb of the left hand now insert the needle at the outside end of the first cross vein and bring the needle out at the point where it meets the central vein but bring the needle out on top of the floss held by your thumb, now insert the needle at the outside end of the next vein on the other side of the central vein and bring it out on top of the thread where the vein meets the central vein and so on till the veins are all put in.

INSTRUCTIONS FOR MAKING RED POPPY DESIGN.

You will require three or four shades of olive-green chenille for the stems, leaves and bulbs and three shades of garnet chenille (poppy tints) for the flowers and buds a little yellowish-green etching silk for the stamens, a skein of seal brown embroidery silk for the French knots, with which to put in the anthers will complete the list of materials. The stems are worked in the satin stitch with the darkest of the three shades of chenille, commence at the bottom of the large stem, giving the chenille the slant indicated by the dotted lines seen in the pattern of the stem, then work the leaves which are made of a medium shade of olive-green chenille. For stitching on the leaves, thread a needle with silk to match the chenille in color and stitch on one-half of the leaf first, and then the other, begining where the leaf joins the stem, stitch on the chenille back and forth from the central vein of the leaf to the outside edge in both cases, giving the chenille the slant indicated by the dotted lines seen in the pattern of the leaves, care being taken to use a lighter shade of chenille for the tips of the leaves, the smaller leaves near the top of the spray are made in a lighter shade as is also the smaller leaves at the bottom.

Begin making the large flower by stitching on the chenille back and forth from the outer edge of the centre circle to the outside edge of the petals, using the lightest shade of garnet chenille, now stitch on an other row of chenille of the medium shade, blending it into the lighter shade, the remaining portion near the centre is then stitched on with the darkest shade, being very careful to keep the ends of the chenille which are near the centre of the flower, closer together than the ends nearer the outside edge, so that the petals will converge towards the centre.

The petals are made to show a little more light garnet chenille near the outside edge, while the three small petals, which are shaded by the green leaves above them, are made with the darkest shades of chenille. almost throughout with the exception of a very few bright layers at the outside edge of each. Now fill in the centre, indicated by the circle seen in the centre of the pattern of the flower, with French knots, using the medium shade of olive-green chenille. This done, thread a needle with yellowish green etching silk and take long stitches from the outside edge of the centre circle to near the outside edge of the petals as indicated by the lines seen in the pattern of the smaller flower, and with the seal brown embroidery silk make a large French knot, at the extreme end of each stitch, this forms the stamens, and anthers, and also completes the flower.

The small flower is made in the same manner, using only the two lighter shades, the inside portion is all made with the brightest shade of garnet-chenille with the exception of a few layers of dark near the top to indicate the shadow caused by the turning over of the petal, the two outside petals are made throughout with the darkest shade with but a few bright layers at the top of the outside upper petal, we will now direct our attention to the bud near the bottom of the spray, the chenille at the point of the bud is darker than the rest and is made with the darkest shade of garnet chenille and the rest of the bud is made with the darkest shade of olive-green chenille, bring the green partly over the lower ends of the garnet, thus giving the red portion of the bud the appearance of peeping out from under the green. Now make the upper bud near the large flower, stitch on the top part with the medium shade of chenille and for that part nearest the bulb, use the darkest shade; when this is done, make the bulb, (that part of the bud nearest the stem,) with the medium shade of olive-green chenille, stitching the green chenille up partly on the red portion of the bud. The bud below this one is made throughout in olive-green chenille with the exception of two or three layers of bright garnet chenille at the point. The bud above the small flower shows but one layer of garnet chenille. Your material is now ready to be made up. Two and a quarter yards of silk ball fringe will be required for trimming and silk pon-pons for the corners. Fringe and pon-pons of varigated garnets would look pretty.

......GUIDE TO......

KENSINGTON * PAINTING,

KENSINGTON OUTLINE

——AND——

OIL PAINTING

——WITH——

BRUSH AND PEN.

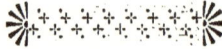

It is the design of the author to give, in an easy and simple manner, such useful and practical instructions to beginners in the art of flower painting as shall enable them to make rapid and satisfactory progress.

In the range of material, objects which attract the attention and now employ the pencil of the artist, none are more inviting than the painting of flowers. Everything which can charm the eye is found to be associated in their forms, elegant, graceful, and varied, giving rise to combinations of light and shade, similarly diversified and charming. These colors, ranging from one end of the chromatic scale to the other, embrace within their scope the most brilliant and gorgeous hues, the tenderest and most delicate tints, while they possess in addition, surface and texture of equally varied characters, thus combining in themselves every physical attribute of that subtle and elusive quality—beauty. It is only surprising that more regard has not hitherto been bestowed upon flower painting. Kensington painting is so called because it is an immitation of the Kensington silk embroideries done with the needle. It is not an easy painting by any means, but work which requires an intimate knowledge of painting, the use of oils, and shading. Of course in all work inferior and tawdry work may be done, whether it be with the brush, pen or needle, but it is possible to produce, and there are being produced constantly, exquisite pieces of Kensington painting by careful workers, which at a distance can scarcely be distinguished from the needle-work they are intended to represent. It is scarcely possible in a written explanation of artistic work, to give as full and complete information as in actual teaching, but if the instructions hereafter given are carefully followed, a good idea of the mode of operation is obtained.

In Kensington painting, the paint used is obtained in tubes, and is the same used for oil painting on canvas. It is better to use the paint as it comes from the tubes without moistening or thining it. The paint is thus purer and gives a heavier and a richer appearance to the work. The paint may sometimes dry, in which case it may be moistened with a drop of linseed oil or turpentine. It is not necessary to have a pallet in using the paints, as a table knife serves the purpose just as well.

The knife is held in the left hand, with the sharp edge towards the worker. The only other articles required to complete the list are two long pointed pens, one smaller and finer than the other for the more delicate work of finishing off, a camels hair brush No. 5, cut square off so that it cannot be rolled to a point, a darning needle No. 18 or 20, and a rather fine needle with the eye-point stuck into a wooden handle to make it firm, and a smooth piece of board to stretch the material upon. With these few simple utensils the operator is ready for work.

Colors used.—Geranium Lake, White, Madder Lake, Emerald-Green, Chrome-Yellow, Raw Sienna, Raw-Umber, Naples-Yellow and Vermilion Red. These are the colors for painting Moss Rose, Wild Rose, Easter Lilies, Wegelia, Poppy, Dasies, Golden Rod, Wheat, Etc., telling what paints to use for each flower, the order in which they are applied, and how to mix them to produce the desired shade in each flower.

The first work to be done after selecting the design you desire to paint, is to make a pattern and stamp the same upon the material, care being taken when the material selected is velvet, that the pile or nap is not too long or thick. Stretch the material upon the board and fasten it with very small tacks. The material must be put on the board without any wrinkles, and if velvet, the pile should be worked down as smooth as possible. It may be surprising to know that most of the painting is done with a tooth pick or pen, placed in a holder the same as for writing, and instead of using a pallet for holding and mixing paints, you use a common table knife. Take a small quantity of the paints you are using and place here and there along the knife, using the knife for holding the paints is one of the secrets of the art, simple as it may appear. If you should use a pallet you will find that when you have a quantity of paint on the pallet and you dip your pen in it, the paint has clgoged the point of your pen so that you cannot see the point. In order to do the work neatly this must never occur. When you are ready to put the paint on the material the paint on the point of the pen should be where the ink would naturally be in writing, on the underside of the pen. In order that the paint may be left only on the underside of the pen, you must use for a pallet something that has a sharp edge, so that by using a knife after you have dipped the pen in the paint you have a desirable edge to draw the edges of the pen over, thereby cleaning the edges of the pen to the point, leaving the paint on the back or in the hollow of the pen. The proper way to work is to hold the knife in the left hand, up from the table, and with the right hand do the painting. You can move the material if you wish, when you have finished one part of a flower, to the position that will be most convenient for yourself, being careful not to rest your hand on the paint you have just put on.

USING THE PEN AND BRUSH.

Hold the pen in your hand the same as for writing, place the point of the pen on the line of the design with the edge side of the pen under, (instead of hollow side as in writing,) with the hollow side of pen facing outside of pattern. Then as you draw the pen toward you in making the stitch, gradually turn the pen so that the hollow side of it would come under, as in writing. The stitches are generally from one-sixteenth to one-eighth of an inch in length. It is difficult to say just how long the stitches should be as they vary in different flowers and different parts of the same flower. It is a very peculiar painting; standing a short distance from the work it looks very much like the Kensington embroidery.

After the outline of the leaf is finished with the pen, representing the outline stitch, the brush is used for filling in the proper shade of the leaf. After the leaf has been painted with the brush between the outlines, the pen is used in as the making the veins of the leaf. The veins are painted to imitate the stitch the same outline. Nearly all the large flowers are made similar to the leaf. The outlines of the flowers and corolla are finished with the pen, also representing the stitch; the filling in between the outlines is done with the brush. Always paint the corolla near the centre, a trifle deeper than the outside or edge of the flower. A great deal of judgment and taste must be exercised in the choice and application of paints, special care being taken to imitate the natural colors of the flowers and leaves.

In making a leaf that has nothing but green in it, nothing but green paint is used The leaves of ferns and the lily-of-the-valley are almost entirely green with a slight touch of yellow or red. Diamond dust may be sprinkled into the paint while it is moist, as it gives a decided improvement to the work. The material is left tacked on the board until the paint is thoroughly dry, when it can be dusted with a wisk without injury.

THE STRUCTURAL ARRANGEMENT OF FLOWERS.

The blossom of a plant or that which is usually denominated a flower, is generally composed of the following distinct parts: The Calyx, so named from a latin word signifying a cup, the Corolla, named from a latin word denoting a crown, the Pericarp is the seed vessel or organ of generation. When coloring a flower or object, use a color the same as the object to be delineated; the outline completed, the next process is to tint in the different local colors. Never work to, but always from the starting point. Properly speaking, there are but three colors in nature, these are red, yellow and blue; they are called primaries, orange, green, purple, and all other hues are only composed from the first three named. The student has then to consider when regarding a color in nature, if it be not one of the primaries, in what proportion it is composed of them. For instance, if orange be the color under consideration, the proper quantities of the red and yellow must be determined by mixing a little of each, adding a little of one or the other until the desired shade is obtained; if green is desired, mix the yellow and blue; a very small portion of red will subdue the brilliancy of green, thus again with purple, which is formed of red and blue, the addition of yellow destroys its purity; in case of orange, blue will destroy or subdue its brilliancy.

If for instance it is desired to make a spray of daisies and a fern on a piece of black velvet on which the design has first been stamped and the material placed on the board as smooth as possible. The white of the daisies is the first thing to make, which is done by placing as much white paint on the knife as will complete the flowers. A small slice of paint is cut from the lump with the coarse pen, then placed upon the knife blade and worked from side to side of the pen, with the hollow part of the pen from the operator, until it is well worked and soft. The point of the pen is then drawn through the paint sidewise until there is a strip of paint in the narrow part of the point of the pen. The operation is begun at the top of the flower by sticking the pen into the pile of the velvet in about the same way that ink is put on paper, and the paint is left as near the top of the leaf as possible. The fine pen is then brought into use in stroking the paint down towards the centre of the flower, with the nibs well opened in so doing. As the flower is naturally darker towards the centre, less paint is worked into it and the dark of the velvet serves as the shade at the bottom of the flower. Care must be taken to put the paint on in large quantities or the flower will look flat and thin and unlike the silk embroidery it is intended to imitate. It takes but little practice until the worker is able to easily imitate the thread-like appearance with the strokes of the pen.

In making the leaves, the brush is used. It is put into a lump of paint of whatever kind is used, and twirled round until it is thick with paint at the point, The brush is then pressed down into the pile of velvet at the top of the leaf, and rolled between the thumb and fore-finger lightly, leaving the paint on the sides, which is afterwards stroked down by the fine pen as in making the flower. When the leaf is small the large pen is used in putting on the paint, but when the leaf is large and it is necessary to put the paint on thickly, the brush can be used to better advantage. It is more difficult to use the brush than the pen, but as the use of the brush expediates the work and a little practice renders the worker proficient in using it, it is better to use it. Sometimes in making leaves, bright colors are required, but instead of putting them on separately, it is better to mix them on the knife blade with the pen and then apply. If for instance a rose leaf is to be made, instead of using all green and then putting in the veins and dark shades with some other paint, it is better to have a little yellow, burnt sienna and Indian red mixed along with the green, and it is then applied with the large pen and stroked with the small one, as was done with the white in making the daisies. This is done in this manner to give the paint the appearance of varied silks. The stems and ferns are made by using the darning needle, which is rolled through the moistened paint until it is thickly covered. It is then passed heavily along the centre of the stem to be made, thus leaving more paint on the sides.

In making the smaller stems and ferns, and all fine work, the small needle is used.

INSTRUCTIONS FOR PAINTING GOLDEN ROD.

The flower is finished first. You can get the light shade of yellow by using chrome-yellow for the dark shades that are put in here and there, use chrome-yellow and raw sienna mixed, also Naples-yellow and raw sienna mixed. The entire flower is finished with the pen, making the stitches irregular, but in such a manner that they will run toward the stems. For the light shades on stems, use emerald-green. It would be well to take your pen and put a stitch on here and there among the flowers, close to the stem, with emerald-green.

INSTRUCTIONS FOR PAINTING WHEAT.

The tops are finished first. You can get the proper shade by using Naples-yellow and white mixed. The tops are made with the pen used in a different manner than you would use it for most all other flowers. You must first get quite a large quantity of paint on the pen, clean the edges on the edge of the knife in the usual way, then, instead of beginning the stitch with the edge of the pen on the material, place the pen squarely on the material, with the hollow side underneath; then press on the pen until it opens so that it will leave paint on both sides of the pen and a trifle in the middle; a stitch in this way forms a grain. The small delicate fibre that projects from the wheat tops is made by the pen with same color as the wheat. The blades are first brushed in with Naples-yellow and white, mixed; the outlines of blades and stems are put on with the pen, using same color as used for the wheat grain; in order to get a green shade for lower blades, mix a little emerald-green with white and yellow, mixed. The outlines and stems and veins are put on with pen in stitch form, using same color as for brushing in the blades.

INSTRUCTIONS FOR PAINTING EASTER-LILY.

Beginning with the bud, to get the pink shade, use a little geranium lake with the white; in painting the open blossom first brush in a little white, then the outlines are put on in white with the pen, to imitate the stitch. The veins are also put on in white; the pistil, projecting from the centre of the flower is put on with the pen using emerald-green at the top of the pistil: the light shade is made by mixing chrome-yellow and white: the stamens are put on in the form of the stitch with the pen, using chrome-yellow, in painting the leaves, brush in chrome-yellow and white mixed. In brushing in the darker shades, use emerald-green mixed with raw sienna; let the brighter shades dry a little before the darker shades are brushed in while you are working on some other part of the design it will dry enought. The outline of the leaf is put on with the pen, representing the stitch: for the bright shades use emerald-green mixed with chrome-yellow or white; for the darker shades use emerald-green mixed with raw sienna. The veins are put on with the pen representing the stitch; for the light colored ones, use Naples-yellow and white; for the dark ones use raw sienna and emerald-green. The stem is put on with the pen, (imitating the stem or outline stitch as nearly as possible) using raw umber and emerald-green.

INSTRUCTIONS FOR PAINTING DAISY.

The corola is finished first. You can get the proper shade by using pure white It is put on with the pen representing the stitch: the centre of the daisy is finished with chrome-yellow and raw sienna for the dark shades, the centre is also finished with the pen to imitate the French knot stitch. In painting the leaves, to get the light shades, use emerald-green and chrome-yellow, for the dark shades use raw sienna. The leaves are painted to represent the stitch. The stems are finished with the same colors and in the same manner as the leaves.

INSTRUCTIONS FOR PAINTING WILD ROSE.

The corola is finished first. Its colors are first brushed in with white and geranium lake, mixed so as make a very bright shade. After you get this shade brushed in, go over it with the pen, making the stitch, using the same color used for brushing in. The centre is made with the pen in stitch form, using for the bright shade, emerald-green and chrome-yellow, and for the darker shade, emerald-green and raw umber. The stamens are made with the pen in stitch form, using chrome-yellow; for darker shades of leaves use raw umber: for the light shades emerald-green mixed with a little chrome-yellow or white; for the dark bud use emerald-green, and chrome-yellow for the lighter shades of the bud: for dark shade on bud, use umber. If you are painting on dark material use the paints given for the light shade on the entire bud. The buds are made with the pen, representing the stitch. Between the stitches scratch in with a sharp tooth-pick or with the back of the pen a little paint of the same shade as the bud. The stems are made with the pen in stem stitch form, using raw sienna and emerald-green.

INSTRUCTIONS FOR PAINTING WEGELIA.

The corola is finished first. By using geranium lake and white mixed, you can produce the proper shade. The centre is finished with the pen representing the stitch. The buds are finished in the same way by using the same colors. In finishing the leaves, first brush in a little Naples-yellow and white mixed; in making the outline of leaves use the pen, making the outlines in the form of a stitch. You can get the proper shade by using emerald-green mixed with Naples-yellow and a little white; for the light brown shades use raw sienna and Naples-yellow; the dark brown shades are made by mixing raw sienna and emerald-green. The veins are made with the pen in stitch form; the stems are brushed in first with Naples-yellow, then go over them with the pen making the stitch and using raw sienna.

INSTRUCTIONS FOR PAINTING MOSS ROSE.

Geranium lake and white mixed, is used for painting the bud or blossom; for painting the darker shades in the flower, use madder lake; the moss is painted with emerald-green, mixing in a little white or yellow to get the lighter shades; to get brown shades, use raw sienna and raw umber. In painting the leaves, brush in with emerald-green mixed with white or yellow to get the different shades. This must be done before the outlines are painted, as all outlines are put on with the pen, representing the stitch. If you should put the outlines on first, when you are filling in with the brush you would be liable to touch the stitches, and your work would not be as neat when finished. In painting the outlines, to get the bright shade, use emerald-green with a little chrome-yellow or white: you can get the dark shade by using raw sienna; if the dark shade is to dark, work in a little Naples-yellow. The same colors are used for the stems as for the moss. The stem, moss rose and bud are all pen work, also veins and outlines of leaf; the filling in of the leaf is done with the brush.

INSTRUCTIONS FOR PAINTING POPPY.

The corola is finished first by brushing in vermilion red. After this is dried, brush in a little madder lake near the lower part of the flower, outside and inside. The outline is put on with the pen in the form of a stitch; the outline and the centre of the flower are all that are put on with the pen; between the outline is brush work. To get the light shades for the outlines, use vermilion red, and for the dark, mix a little madder lake. The stems are put on with the pen by using white, put on lightly with the edge of the pen. For the centre of the flower below the stems, use emerald-green; the leaves are brushed in with emerald-green mixed with white or Naples-yellow.